— OUTDOOR ADVENTURE GUIDES —

WILDLIFE WATCHING

Spotting Animals on Outdoor Adventures

by Raymond Bean

Consultant: Gabriel J. Gassman
Outdoor Professional

CAPSTONE PRESS
a capstone imprint

Capstone Captivate is published by Capstone Press, an imprint of Capstone.
1710 Roe Crest Drive
North Mankato, Minnesota 56003
www.capstonepub.com

Copyright © 2020 Capstone. All rights reserved. No part of this publication may be reproduced in whole or in part, or stored in a retrieval system, or transmitted in any form or by any means, electronic, mechanical, photocopying, recording, or otherwise, without written permission of the publisher.

Cataloging-in-Publication Data is available on the Library of Congress website.
ISBN: 978-1-5435-9035-7 (library binding)
ISBN: 978-1-4966-6618-5 (paperback)
ISBN: 978-1-5435-9036-4 (eBook PDF)

Summary: This guidebook provides basic tips and tricks for wildlife spotting and nature photography, including recognizing animal signs, packing essential gear, and following wildlife do's and don'ts.

Editorial Credits
Editor: Kellie M. Hultgren; Designer: Juliette Peters;
Media Researcher: Morgan Walters; Production Specialist: Katy LaVigne

Photo Credits
Getty Images: Jacob W. Frank, 16; iStockphoto: FatCamera, 36, fstop123, 42, pabst_ell, 33, SolStock, 40; Juliette Peters, 28, top left 39, bottom left 39; Shutterstock: , AIVRAD, (spray) 12, aliaksei kruhlenia, (icons) design element, all_about_people, bottom 10, axeiz, 15, BlueOrange Studio, 38, Bodor Tivadar, (prints) 37, Chantelle Bosch, 18, Daboost, (book) 37, Debbie Steinhausser, 23, Diane079F, 4, Dmitry Pichugin, 17, Doug McLean, bottom right Cover, Duplass, top 10, Emily Veinglory, bottom right 26, FloridaStock, 31, Giedriius, 6, hd connelly, 12, Hellen Grig, top right 39, Irina Papoyan, 30, Jay Ondreicka, top right 13, Jeff Whyte, 7, Jeffrey J Davis, 29, Joebite, (case) bottom 39, Keith Bell, (trail camera) top left 35, Kirk Geisler, top Cover, kronnui, (grass) background Cover, Malgorzata Surawska, 24, Maria Evseyeva, 25, Matauw, top right 27, Max Allen, top left 26, moosehenderson, top left 13, New Africa, 14, r.classen, (forest) design element, Serg64, bottom right 39, She Homesteads, 21, shutter_o, (moss) design element, Spreewald-Birgit, 22, Steve Collender, (tape) design element, suriya yapin, bottom left Cover, Tony Campbell, 1, 11, trattieritratti, 41, Treetops Interactive, 19, VBVVCTND, (khaki) design element, Vickey Chauhan, top 35, Viktor Loki, middle left 27, Vishnevskiy Vasily, 5, VP Photo Studio, 9, 45, vz maze, 32, Ysbrand Cosijn, 20

All internet sites appearing in back matter were available and accurate when this book was sent to press.

TABLE OF CONTENTS

CHAPTER 1
ANIMALS ALL AROUND YOU 4

CHAPTER 2
SAFETY 8

CHAPTER 3
BE AN ANIMAL DETECTIVE 14

CHAPTER 4
BE PATIENT, STILL, AND QUIET 28

CHAPTER 5
NEXT-LEVEL WILDLIFE WATCHING 34

MAKE YOUR OWN
WILDLIFE-WATCHING KIT 44

GLOSSARY 46
READ MORE 47
INTERNET SITES 47
INDEX 48

Words in **bold** are in the glossary.

CHAPTER 1
ANIMALS ALL AROUND YOU

Have you ever spotted a rabbit running across the yard or a hawk circling overhead? If you get excited when you see wild animals, you're not alone. Watching a beautiful creature in its natural **habitat** is a thrill.

Wildlife watching takes patience. But if you know where, when, and how to look, there's a lot to see! Start with the animals that live near humans.

BACKYARD CRITTERS

What animals live near you? Sit quietly in a park or yard, and you might catch a glimpse. Birds are easy to find in most places. Squirrels, chipmunks, groundhogs, and rabbits often live near humans. Deer live near fields and forests where they can hide. Watch for them at dawn and dusk.

WATCH WISELY

Use these tips to watch and identify birds:

 Listen for their unique calls.

 Take photographs so you can look them up online or at the library.

 Look for bird-watching tours in your city or town. Your local National Audubon Society branch is a good place to start.

UNEXPECTED SIGHTS

Many places seem to have only common backyard animals. If you look a little closer, though, you might be surprised. Some cities are home to foxes, coyotes, eagles, and other **predators**. These animals eat smaller animals that live near humans. Raccoons and opossums will snack on humans' garbage and gardens. Turtles, frogs, and toads hide near water. Snakes are shy, but they live in many different places.

Don't wait until you're on an outdoor adventure to **observe** animals. Practice watching animals that live near you. Soon you'll be ready to find them in the wild!

CITY SURPRISES

Some cities are wilder than you think. Who would have thought these animals are city slickers?

❑ Hundreds of California sea lions hang out at Pier 39 in San Francisco, California.

❑ More than a million bats spend summers at the Ann W. Richards Congress Avenue Bridge in Austin, Texas.

❑ Migrating salmon swim over a fish ladder in Seattle, Washington, each year.

❑ Turkeys and their babies often stop traffic in Minneapolis, Minnesota.

CHAPTER 2
SAFETY

Safety is the most important part of wildlife watching. Wild animals are, well, wild! Give animals your respect. You will be safer and happier, and so will they.

THE BASICS

▶ Stick together. Never go into the wild alone. If you get injured or lost, you'll need someone else to help.

▶ Plan ahead. Check with park rangers to make sure you understand the rules.

▶ Keep your distance. Don't get too close to a wild animal. You or the animal might get hurt.

WATCH WISELY

It's best to leave dogs at home when wildlife watching. Dogs can chase or scare away other animals. And some wild animals can hurt dogs. If you do bring a dog, always keep it on a leash.

LEAVE NOTHING BEHIND

When you're out in the wild, clean up after yourself. Food and trash can invite animals into areas where they shouldn't be. When animals learn that humans often have food, they can lose their fear of people. Some animals might even attack people to get food.

Human food can also make animals sick. And animals can't tell the difference between food and plastic or foil wrappers. When animals eat wrappers, they can get very sick or even die. Clean up to keep animals safe!

WATCH WISELY
Never crowd or chase an animal. A frightened animal might bite.

BABY ANIMALS

Baby animals are super cute! But if you spot them, give them lots of space. Keep these tips in mind:

★ Stay very quiet so you don't scare the animals.
★ Never try to touch or pick up baby animals.
★ Never get between a baby animal and its parent.
★ If a baby animal seems lost or abandoned, watch closely. Its parent is probably nearby.
★ Adult animals are very protective of babies. If they think you are a threat, they might attack you.
★ When you are done observing, move slowly out of the area to safety.
★ If you see a baby bear alone, it's safest to leave right away. Go back the way you came.

ANIMAL DANGERS

What should you do if you cross paths with a dangerous animal? Stay calm. Move slowly. Stand up tall and try to look larger than you really are.

Most animals are as afraid of you as you are of them. But always be careful. Here are some tips for getting away from some common dangerous animals.

BEARS

- If you're going to a place known to have bears, bring bear spray. Make lots of noise as you hike to warn bears away from you.

- If you see a bear, stay calm. Most bear encounters do not end in injury.

- Quietly warn others in your group about the bear.

- Stick together. As a group, you'll appear larger to the bear.

- Back away, slowly, in the direction from which you came.

- Don't run. A bear will chase animals that run away. And it's faster than you are!

- Keep your eyes on the bear. It will probably want to get away from you too.

MOUNTAIN LIONS

▶ Stand tall and wave your jacket or pack around to look bigger than you are.

▶ If you're in a group, get close together.

▶ Make noise. Shout or bang on your gear, or blow an air horn.

▶ Do not run. If it thinks you are prey, it will chase you.

SNAKES

▶ Remember that most snakes will not attack if they are not threatened.

▶ Don't try to touch it or drive it away with sticks or noise.

▶ Give the snake plenty of space and leave the area.

▶ Avoid most snakes by staying on paths.

CHAPTER 3
BE AN ANIMAL DETECTIVE

How can you find animals to observe? Look for the signs they leave behind. Like a detective, you can find the clues and figure out what animals are around.

GEAR

You already have the most important tools for wildlife watching: your eyes and ears! But gathering some gear can help.

GEAR CHECKLIST

❑ Field journal—to record your sightings, measurements, and questions

❑ Smartphone or digital camera—to keep track of what you see and look up more information later

❑ Field guide to animal **tracks**—to figure out if you're following a bunny or a bobcat

❑ List of local animals—to help identify what you see

❑ Magnifying glass—to get a close-up view of signs that animals leave behind

❑ Measuring tape—to measure footprints and other signs of an animal visit

❑ Binoculars—to zoom in on a distant critter without startling it

TRACKS

Tracks are animal footprints. If you know what to look for, they can tell you what animals are around and where they live.

Get up early in the morning to look for tracks. Look at the ground as you walk around slowly. Fresh snow and soft soil, such as mud and sand, are perfect for spotting tracks.

wolf tracks

When you find a track, think like a detective. Ask yourself some questions. Where was the animal coming from? Where was it going? Why do you think that? How long ago did it visit the area? Where might it be now? Look around you. Is the animal nearby?

bear tracks

IDENTIFYING TRACKS

Once you find a track, think about what kind of animal might have made it. The track probably fits into one of three groups:

▶ If the track looks like a bunch of connected lines, it was probably made by a bird.

▶ If the track resembles a paw or hoof and you can make out claw or toe imprints, it was probably made by a **mammal**.

▶ A track that doesn't fit one of the first two categories may have been made by a reptile, amphibian, or insect.

WILDLIFE TRACKS

TRAILS AND TUNNELS

If you don't find tracks, what other clues can you find? Animals leave other signs too. Look for anything that seems different from the area around it.

Animals like to take the same **trails** over and over again. A trail might look like a clear path through tall grass or bushes. Grass or twigs along the trail may be bent or broken. If an animal likes to lie down or hide in a spot, the earth or leaves might be flattened there.

Some animals use tunnels to move from one place to another in safety. To find a tunnel, look for holes or trenches just beneath the surface. Some tunnels go into the dirt, and others go under grass and fallen leaves. You might see lumps in the ground above a tunnel. Look carefully, but never stick anything into a tunnel!

ANIMAL HOMES

If you follow tracks, trails, and tunnels, you may find animals' homes. Most animal homes are hard to find. The animals don't want to be bothered. Knowing what to look for will give you clues about who lives there.

NESTS

Birds, squirrels, and other tree-dwelling animals live in nests. These nests are usually made of grass, twigs, and leaves woven together in a circle. Most are shaped like bowls or balls. A field guide will tell you what probably made each kind of nest.

BURROWS

Some animals live in **burrows**. These underground homes protect them from predators and weather. If you find the entrance to a burrow, think about the size of the animal that made it. Small animals, such as rabbits or chipmunks, make small holes. Larger holes are made by larger animals, such as foxes or otters.

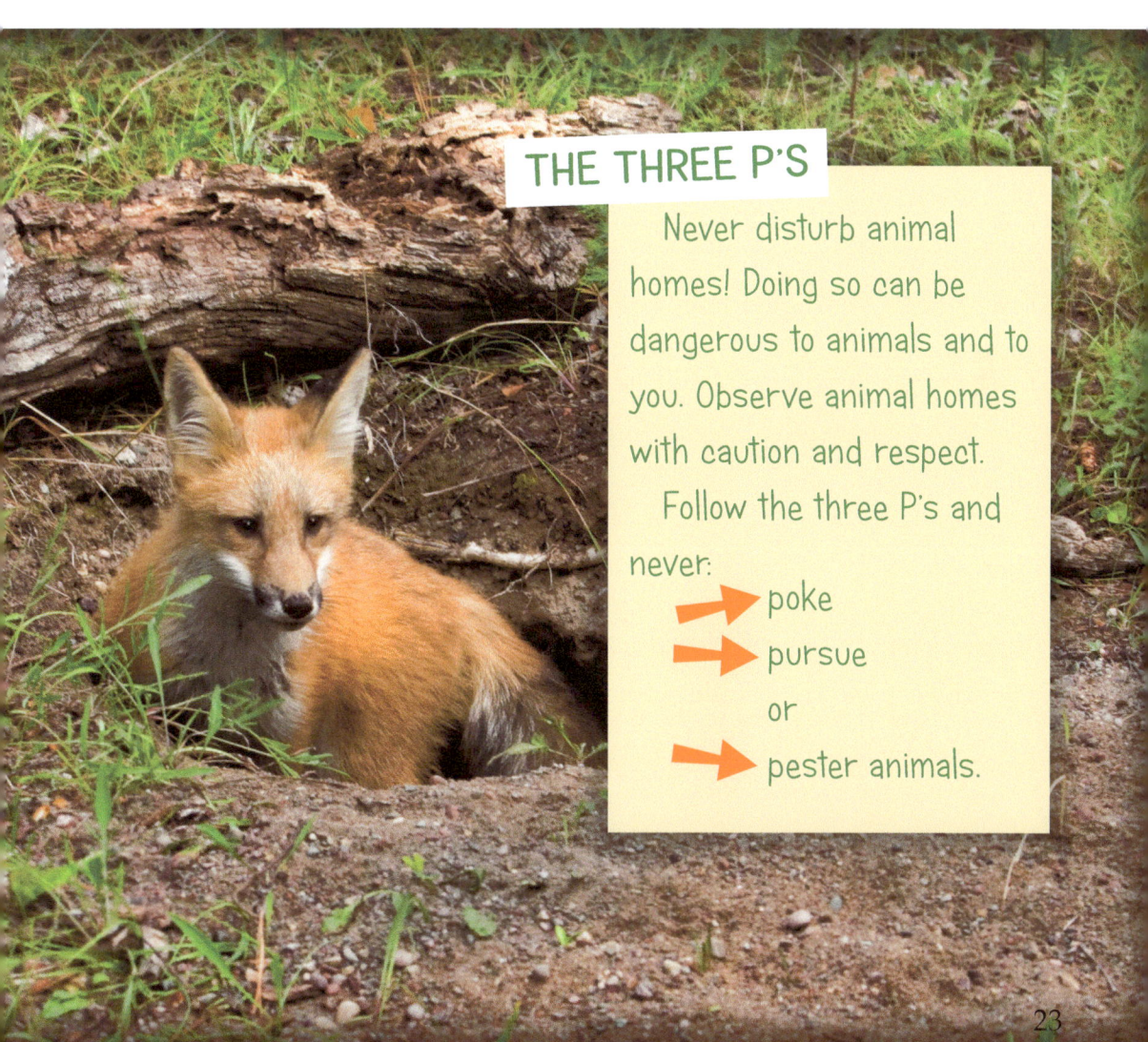

THE THREE P'S

Never disturb animal homes! Doing so can be dangerous to animals and to you. Observe animal homes with caution and respect.

Follow the three P's and never:
- poke
- pursue or
- pester animals.

SIGNS OF FEEDING

Animals often leave signs that they've been snacking. Look for bite and chew marks on twigs, branches, bark, and leaves.

Some clues can tell you what animals have stopped for a bite:

Twigs that look broken at the top and are cut at a 45-degree angle are signs of deer or rabbits.

Parallel grooves on branches often show that rabbits or rodents have been nibbling.

Small piles or scatterings of nut or seed shells might have been left by squirrels, chipmunks, or birds.

BE A DETECTIVE

When wildlife watching, be a detective and do the following:

1. **Trust your instincts:** If something seems important, it probably is.
2. **Observe:** Pay attention to every detail around you.
3. **Record:** What do you see? Write down your observations to help you figure out what animals might be in the area.
4. **Think:** How do the clues you've noticed fit together to tell the story of what is going on?

SCAT

One of the most helpful clues for finding animals in the wild is also the grossest. Every animal leaves **scat**, or poop. And animals don't have toilets, so you'll find their number-twos outside if you look carefully.

bobcat scat

Long, thick, tubelike scat is usually left by a dog, coyote, fox, bobcat, or other **carnivore**. You might see bits of fur, bone, or scales in it. It usually smells awful!

Piles of round, pellet-shaped scat come from a deer, rabbit, or other **herbivore**. It doesn't smell much, and you might see bits of plant material in it.

rabbit scat

WATCH WISELY

If the scat contains hair, it probably came from a predator.

White scat usually comes from a bird or reptile.

goose scat

bear scat

Pile-shaped scat is often left by a bear, cow, or buffalo.

GROSS FACTOR

When observing scat, follow three safety rules.

1. Don't touch it! Scat can contain dangerous germs and **bacteria**.

2. Don't step in it! Getting scat on your shoes or gear can spread germs.

3. Breathe through your mouth to cut down on the smell.

CHAPTER 4
BE PATIENT, STILL, AND QUIET

You have followed the clues. What should you do when wildlife is close? The goal is to see the animals' natural **behavior**. That is easiest when the animals don't know you're there.

First, be patient. Find a comfortable spot and settle in for a while. Listen to the sounds of life around you. It may take twenty minutes or more before the animals get used to you and start moving again. If animals don't appear, don't rush to the next spot.

Once you're settled, be still. Don't dig in your bag or wander around. Too much noise or movement will scare critters away.

Finally, be silent. Don't talk to yourself, others, or the animals. Even whispers can send animals away from you. If you brought a phone, turn its sounds off.

USE YOUR SENSES

As you are patient, still, and silent, use your senses. The animals around you surely are!

Sight: Scan the area around you slowly. Allow your eyes to rest on a location for a while. Animals are often hiding in plain sight. Your eyes need time to adjust and see what's right in front of you.

Sound: After a few minutes of silence, you'll begin to hear even the slightest sounds. Listen for animal sounds and the rustling of leaves and branches.

Smell: You might be able to smell scat, urine, **musk**, or other animal scents.

COMMON ANIMAL SOUNDS

When wildlife watching, listen for these common animal sounds.

- Owls, doves, and many birds make *woot* sounds.
- Woodpeckers at work sound like hammering.
- Coyotes, wildcats, foxes, and other predators howl, yowl, and bark.
- Birds and many ground animals, such as chipmunks, chirp and squeak.
- Large animals, such as moose and bears, may not make much noise. But you can often hear the rustling they make as they move.
- Turtles, fish, and other water creatures make small splashes.

YOU SMELL!

No offense, but you smell! Most animals will smell you before you see them. The wind carries your scent to animals you haven't seen yet.

When you settle in to watch, try to stay downwind from where you think animals might be. Find a place where the wind will pass the animal before it passes you. Your scent will move away from the animal instead of toward it.

WATCH WISELY

Don't wear strong scents, including soaps, lotions, and sprays. Wear clothes in colors that blend into the area. Always have a camera or video recorder ready to go. If you spot an animal, stay calm. Sudden movements or sounds will startle the animal and send it running.

CHAPTER 5
NEXT-LEVEL WILDLIFE WATCHING

Modern wildlife watchers have many fun tools. You can invite wildlife to come to you or view it at a distance. Read on for ways to level up your skills.

WILD TECH

Technology can help the curious wildlife watcher. If you use a mobile device, check out some wildlife apps. With an adult's help, research apps that can help you identify critters and keep track of your sightings.

CHOOSE YOUR APP

Useful apps will:
➡ provide examples of tracks and sounds.
➡ have a place to record your sightings and take notes.
➡ let you snap a picture of a track or animal and upload it.

Trail cameras can observe shy or dangerous creatures without disturbing them. These tools snap photos or take video of wild animals. When animals pass by, a motion sensor turns the camera on. Motion cameras never get bored or fall asleep. Some can even take pictures in the dark!

WATCH WISELY

Most parks do not allow the use of private trail cameras. Check park websites for animal camera feeds instead.

RECORD YOUR OBSERVATIONS

Now that you have observed wild animals, record what you saw in the wild. A field journal will help you keep track of what you see from season to season and year to year. A plain paper notebook and pencil are all you need.

As you watch for wildlife, keep your notebook open. Write down the date and time. When you spot an animal, make notes right away. Record as many details as possible. Write down questions you have.

Monday, August 12
Today I saw tracks in the mud near the edge of the woods in the backyard. They looked like this:

It looks like the animal moved across the lawn and was headed into the woods.

The tracks show that the animal has sharp nails or claws. I think it is a raccoon track.

I searched for scat but couldn't find any.

I found similar tracks in the area the last time it rained.

Could this be the raccoon that ate the tomatoes in the garden?

If you see the animal, sketch it in your notebook. If you use a camera, leave a space in the notebook for pictures. You can print them out and paste them in when you get home.

TAKING PICTURES IN THE WILD

Taking photos of clues and wildlife is a great way to record your observations. Make a scrapbook of your wildlife sightings or create a photo slideshow on the computer. Photos also let you take nature home with you without hurting animals or their habitats.

As you track wildlife, move slowly. Look closely at the world around you. Sometimes the most amazing photos are of things you normally wouldn't even notice. A close-up of a gnawed twig or animal print can help you identify critters at home. And you can make really cool art!

WATCH WISELY

If you're using a mobile phone to take pictures, buy a waterproof pouch. If you drop your phone in water or get caught in the rain, it will be protected.

FINDING OTHER WILDLIFE WATCHERS

You're not the only animal lover in town. A club or group in your area might meet to share knowledge and plan trips. Together, you might learn more, see more wildlife, and even make new friends.

▶ The National Audubon Society works to protect birds and their habitats. It is named after John James Audubon, a famous naturalist and artist.

▶ The National Wildlife Foundation protects wild animals and the places they live.

▶ The National Park Service helps protect and maintain U.S. national parks. Wildlife of all kinds can live undisturbed in these areas.

▶ Your local park may offer clubs or programs for watching wildlife.

If you want to get even closer to wildlife, think about volunteering at a park or wildlife club. Talk to an adult about what you can do. Whether you clean up a park, build bat or bird boxes, or even help injured animals heal, you are helping wildlife thrive.

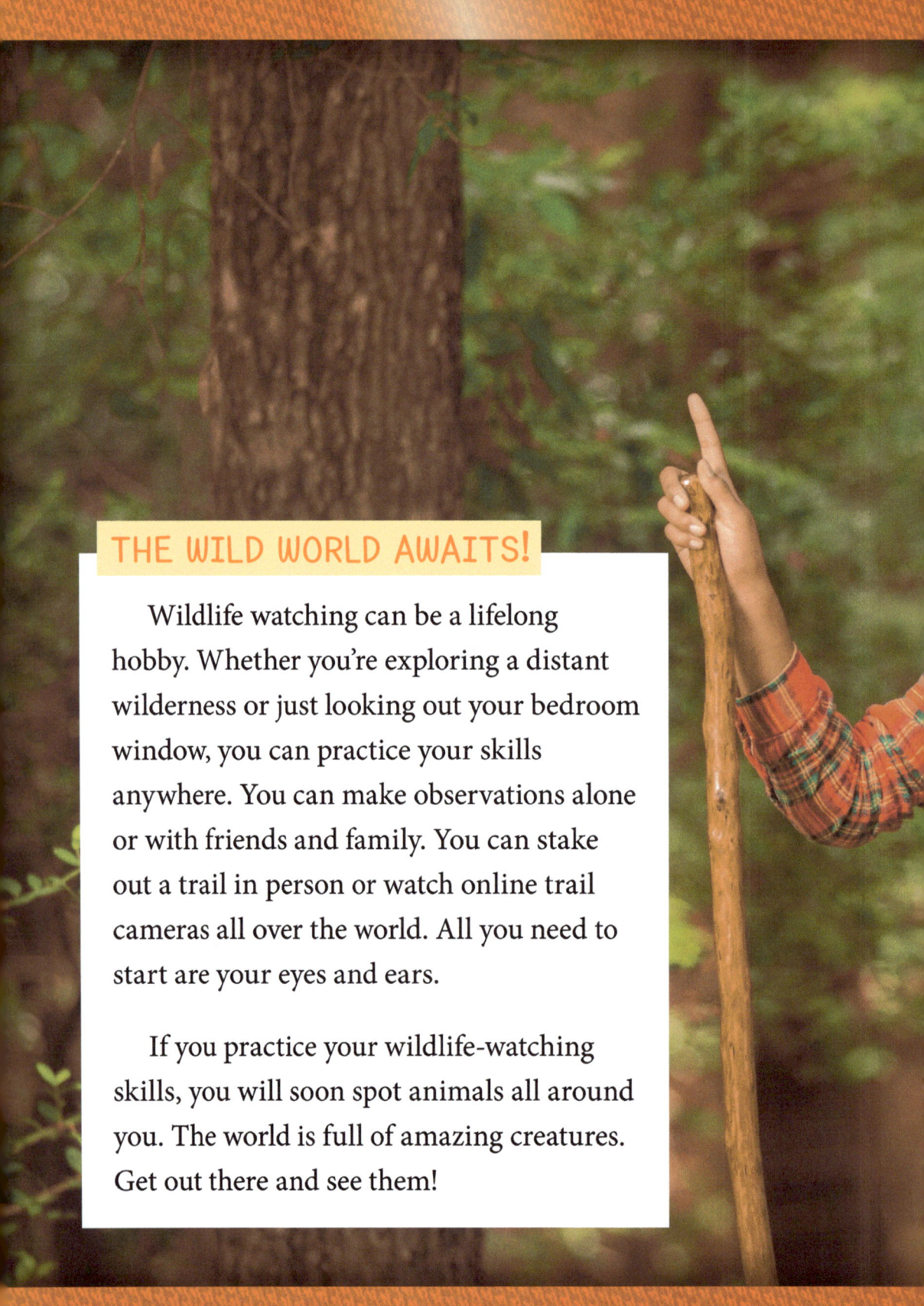

THE WILD WORLD AWAITS!

Wildlife watching can be a lifelong hobby. Whether you're exploring a distant wilderness or just looking out your bedroom window, you can practice your skills anywhere. You can make observations alone or with friends and family. You can stake out a trail in person or watch online trail cameras all over the world. All you need to start are your eyes and ears.

If you practice your wildlife-watching skills, you will soon spot animals all around you. The world is full of amazing creatures. Get out there and see them!

MAKE YOUR OWN WILDLIFE-WATCHING KIT

Prepare for your next wildlife-watching adventure with this list. The right tools will help you spot new animals and record your findings. Before you go, be sure to pack:

BASICS:
- camera or smartphone—for capturing video and photos of wildlife
- field journal and pencil—to record clues as you crack the case of what lives in the area
- first-aid kit—in case of cuts or scrapes
- water bottle—to stay hydrated as you watch

WATCH WISELY

If you are in an area with bears or other dangerous wildlife, bring bear spray and an air horn. You can never be too safe in the wild!

NEXT-LEVEL KIT:
- ❏ animal identification book or app—to look up what you see
- ❏ animal tracks guide—to look up tracks and the animals that make them
- ❏ binoculars—for observing animals at a safe distance
- ❏ clothing in muted greens and browns—to help you blend in
- ❏ magnifying glass—to get a closer look at chewed vegetation, tracks, and even scat
- ❏ measuring tape—to measure tracks, holes, and other signs
- ❏ scat guide—not all poo will look the same to you!

GLOSSARY

bacteria (bak-TIR-ee-ah)—microscopic organisms that live in soil, water, and the bodies of plants and animals; some can cause disease.

behavior (be-HAYV-yor)—how something acts

burrow (BUR-oh)—a hole or tunnel where an animal lives or hides

carnivore (CAR-ni-vor)—an animal that eats only meat

habitat (HAB-i-tat)—the place where a plant or animal normally lives

herbivore (HER-bih-vor)—an animal that eats only plants

mammal (MAM-ull)—a warm-blooded animal that has hair and feeds its young on milk

musk (MUHSK)—a strongly scented substance that some animals produce to mark where they live

observe (ub-SERV)—to watch and learn about

predator (PRED-uh-tor)—an animal that eats other animals

scat (skat)—animal poop

tracks (TRAKS)—prints from an animal's feet, tail, or other body part

trail (TRAYL)—a path made by animals

READ MORE

Brooklyn Botanic Garden. *The Kid's Guide to Exploring Nature.* Brooklyn, NY: Brooklyn Botanic Garden, 2015.

Carwardine, Mark, and Amy-Jane Beer. *Lonely Planet's A–Z of Wildlife Watching.* Oakland, CA: Lonely Planet, 2018.

Posada, Mia. *Who Was Here?: Discovering Wild Animal Tracks.* Minneapolis: Millbrook Press, 2014.

Townsend, John. *Life-Sized Animal Tracks.* Brighton, UK: Book House, 2018.

INTERNET SITES

Cornell Lab of Ornithology
https://ebird.org

National Audubon Society
https://www.audubon.org

National Wildlife Federation: Ranger Rick
https://rangerrick.org

INDEX

apps, 34, 45

baby animals, 7, 11
backyard animals, 4
bats, 7, 41
bears, 11, 12, 27, 31, 44
behavior, 28
binoculars, 15, 45
birds, 4, 5, 19, 22, 24, 27, 31, 41
bobcats, 15, 26
burrows, 23

carnivores, 26
chipmunks, 4, 23, 24, 31
cleanup, 10, 41
clothes, 32, 45
clubs, 40–41
coyotes, 6, 26, 31

deer, 4, 24, 26
dogs, 8, 26

feeding signs, 24
field guides, 15, 22
field journals, 15, 36–37, 44
fish, 7, 31
food, 10
foxes, 6, 23, 26, 31

gear, 14–15, 44–45

herbivores, 26

mobile devices, 34, 39
mountain lions, 13

nests, 22

opossums, 6

photos, 5, 35, 38–39, 44
planning, 8, 40
predators, 6, 23, 26, 31

rabbits, 4, 15, 23, 24, 26
raccoons, 6
rangers, 8

safety, 8, 10, 11, 23, 27, 44
scat, 26–27, 30, 45
scents, 30, 32, 33
sea lions, 7
snakes, 6, 13
sounds, 30, 31, 32, 34
squirrels, 4, 22, 24

tracks, 15, 16, 19, 22, 34
trail cameras, 35
trails, 20, 22, 42
trash, 10
tunnels, 21, 22
turkeys, 7
turtles, 6, 31

volunteering, 41

websites, 35
wildlife-watching kit, 44–45